NICE & SOUTHERN FRANCE TRAVEL GUIDE

Journey Through French Riviera, Avignon, Aix-en-Provence, Marseille, Nimes And Southern France. Best places To Visit In 2023 2024 And Beyond

Jette Florence

Copyright © 2023 by *Jette Florence*

All rights reserved. No part of this publication may be reproduced, distributed, or transmitted in any form or by any means, including photocopying, recording, or other electronic or mechanical methods. All Rights Reserved.

Table Of Contents

Embarking On The Journey Of Enchantment............7

Chapter 1...............10

Introduction To Southern France..........10

- The Allure Of Southern France..............10
- Getting To Southern France..............11
- Getting Around Southern France..............12
- An Overview Of The Regions..............14
- Weather And Best Seasons To Visit..............15
- Travelers' Cultural Etiquette And Tips..............16
- Tips For Creating a Travel Budget..............17

Basic French Phrases..............18

- Greetings and Introductions..............19
- Basic Communications..............20
- Asking for Directions..............21
- Basic Expressions..............21
- Farewells..............22

Chapter 2..............24

Marseille's Coastal Splendors And Urban Charms..............24

- Hello And Welcome To Marseille..............24
- Visiting the Old Port and the Le Panier District.......25
- Adventure in the Calanques National Park..............26
- Museums and markets..............26
- Where to Eat and Drink..............27

Options for lodging...28
Marseille 3 Days Itinerary.. 28

Chapter 3...33
Nice Riviera Elegance And Mediterranean Bliss.................................... 33

The French-Riviera's Allure..................................... 33
Cultural Diversity and Historical Importance...........34
The Mediterranean Climate and Its Implications.... 35
Nice' 3 Days Itinerary...35

Chapter 4...42
Avignon - Papal History and Provençal Delights... 42

Discovering Avignon's Allure................................. 43
Exploring Luberon Villages..................................... 43
Traditional Provençal Flavors................................. 44
Avignon Relaxation..45
3 Days Itinerary For Avignon................................. 46

Chapter 5...51
Montpellier - Modern Energy and Medieval Roots..51

Montpellier Unveiled... 51
Historic Streets and Eclectic Architecture...............51
Languedoc Wine Tasting and Local Cuisine...........52
La Grande Motte Beach Escape.............................53
Accommodation for Everyone................................54
Montpellier Itinerary.. 55

Chapter 6.. 61

Aix-en Provence - Art, Culture, and Sophistication 61
- Introducing Aix-en-Provence 61
- Cours Mirabeau and Museums Galore 62
- Exploring Local Markets and Cézanne's Trails 63
- A Gourmet Escape Through Aix's Culinary Scene. 64
- Where To Stay 64
- Itinerary for Aix-en-Provence 65

Chapter 7 69
Arles's Ancient Heritage and Van Gogh's Legacy 69
- Roman Ruins and Van Gogh Walking Tour in Arles ... 70
- Exploration of the Camargue and Wildlife Encounters 71
- From Bistros to Riverside Cafés, Dining on the Rhône 72
- Finding Rest In Cozy Guest Houses And Historic Inns 73
- 2 Days Itinerary for Arles 74

Chapter 8 77
Nimes, The Roman Grandeur And Southern Charisma 77
- Nimes Fascinates! 77
- Amphitheatre and Maison Carrée 78
- Jardins de la Fontaine and Local Markets 79
- Nîmoise Delicacies And Culinary Temptations 79
- Accommodation Options 80

Nimes Itinerary..81

Chapter 9..85
Hidden Treasures and Countryside Getaways... 85
Beyond the Main Cities................................85
Rustic Villages.. 85
Côtes du Rhône Wine Route Adventure................87
Relaxation in Saint-Rémy-de-Provence...................88
Budget-Friendly Charm...88
Itinerary for the Hidden Treasures and Countryside Getaways...89

Chapter 10..94
Useful Informations For Tourist.............94
Trends And Highlights To Look Forward-To............94
Travel Trends...94
Highlights to be expected..................................... 95
Essential Websites, Apps, Maps and Travel Resources..96
Making Your Own Customized Itinerary................. 97

Tourist Information Centres.................. 100
Office de Tourisme de Nice....................................100
Marseille Tourist Office.. 100
Office de Tourisme de Bordeaux Métropole.......... 100
Toulouse Tourist Office... 101
Avignon Tourist Office.. 101
Cannes Tourist Office... 101
Aix-en-Provence Tourist Office............................... 101
Montpellier Tourist Office....................................... 102

Embarking On The Journey Of Enchantment

Dear Travelers,

Welcome to the pages of these "Nice and Southern France Travel Guide." As you hold this book in your hands, you are not merely flipping through pages filled with words and sceneries. You are setting your foot on a path of discovery, an odyssey through the heart and soul of one of the most enchanting regions in the world.

In these pages, you'll find more than just directions and recommendations. You'll uncover the stories woven into the cobblestone streets, the fragrance of lavender fields carried by the gentle Provençal breeze, and the warmth of sunsets casting their golden glow on the azure Mediterranean waters.

This guide is a labor of love, born from a profound appreciation for the rich tapestry that is Nice and Southern France. It's for the wanderers who yearn to explore beyond the obvious, the dreamers who seek to immerse themselves in the colors, flavors, and rhythms of this vibrant land.

Whether you're strolling through historic cities, indulging in gastronomic delights, or basking in the cultural heritage that stretches across every village and town, this guide is your trusted companion.

With each page turned, you're embarking on a journey that transcends the boundaries of time and space. The pages may be static, but the experiences they describe are alive with the essence of this wondrous region.

From the elegance of Nice's Promenade des Anglais to the rugged beauty of the Provencal countryside, you're about to step into a world that leaves an indelible mark on your heart.

As you follow these words, know that you're not alone in your exploration. Every recommendation, every piece of advice, and every anecdote herein is shared with the intention of enhancing your adventure.

Let this guide be the compass that points you toward the unforgettable, the unexpected, and the unparalleled.

So, with curiosity as your guide and the "Nice and Southern France Travel Guide" in your hands, let the journey begin. May your travels be filled with awe, wonder, and moments that linger in your memory long after you've returned home.

Bon voyage!

Jette Florence

NICE & SOUTHERN FRANCE TRAVEL GUIDE 2023

Chapter 1

Introduction To Southern France

The Allure Of Southern France

Southern France, often known as the "Midi" or "Sud de la France," is a mesmerizing region that draws visitors with its rich history, magnificent landscapes, and dynamic culture.

From the sun-kissed beaches of the Mediterranean to the quaint Provençal villages found among fragrant lavender fields, this region has something for every sort of traveler.

Imagine meandering down centuries-old cobblestone alleyways, indulging in excellent cuisine, and immersing yourself in an artistic tradition that has inspired numerous artists, writers, and thinkers.

Southern France's attractiveness stems from its seamless blend of past and present, where modern amenities coexist with a tangible link to its historic history.

Getting To Southern France

Mediterranean beaches, medieval cities, and delectable cuisine make this a popular tourist destination. Here's a step-by-step guide on getting to southern France from another country:

Select your preferred Arrival Airport
Southern France has a number of large airports that serve as entry points for international visitors. Among the most notable are:

- Nice Côte d'Azur Airport (NCE) is located in Nice.
- Marseille Provence Airport (MRS) is located in Marseille.
- Toulouse-Blagnac Airport (TLS) is located in Toulouse, France.

Purchase Flights
Begin by researching and reserving flights to one of the airports listed above. To find the greatest rates and possibilities, you can use internet travel platforms, airline websites, or travel bureaus.

Consider things like trip dates, layovers, and total flight duration.

Obtain Required Travel Documents
Make sure you have a valid passport as well as any necessary visas for your trip to France. Check the exact requirements for your nationality and duration of stay.

Create an Itinerary
Determine the cities or regions in southern France you want to visit. Nice, Cannes, Marseille, Aix-en-Provence, Avignon, and the French Riviera are all popular tourist attractions.

Don't know how to get about your personal itinerary? Well, Good news! I have compiled a thorough itinerary for all of the aforementioned places in each chapter of this book!

Getting Around Southern France

When you arrive in Nice, you will find good public transportation options such as buses, trams, and trains to get about the city and to neighboring regions.

The Nice Airport Express Bus, tram line, or taxis make it easy to get to the city center from the airport.

You can take a shuttle bus from Marseille Airport to the neighboring Marseille Saint-Charles train station. This station connects to cities around the region and beyond.

To explore the nearby districts, you can also take cabs, ride-sharing services, or hire a car at the airport.

Toulouse-Blagnac International Airport (TLS)

To get to the city center from Toulouse Airport, utilize the tramway or the airport shuttle.

Toulouse is well-connected by train and bus, making it simple to travel around southern France.

Transportation

Trains, buses, and trams are commonly available and efficient modes of public transportation for traveling around within cities and between communities in the region.

Rental cars

If you want to visit numerous locations, renting a car may be more convenient, especially for getting to more rural spots.
For local mobility, taxis and ride-sharing options are also available.

An Overview Of The Regions

Southern France stretches from the scenic Pyrenees foothills along the Spanish border to the fashionable French Riviera and the azure coastlines of the Mediterranean Sea.

This region's geography is diverse, with coastal havens, luscious vineyards, undulating hills, and even severe mountain regions.

Most Notable Cities In Southern France Include

Marseille

Marseille is France's second-largest city, known for its bustling port, colorful marketplaces, and cultural fusion influenced by its role as a melting pot of Mediterranean civilizations.

Nice

Located on the French Riviera, Nice features beautiful beaches, a picturesque ancient town, and a mix of French and Italian architectural influences.

Toulouse

Known as "La Ville Rose" (The Pink City) because of its terracotta structures, Toulouse is a center of aerospace and technology industries, as well as an arts and culture center.

Avignon

Avignon is famous for its stunning Palais des Papes (Palace of the Popes) and historical significance as the papal residence in the 14th century.

Weather And Best Seasons To Visit

Southern France enjoys a Mediterranean climate with moderate, rainy winters and hot, dry summers. The best time to visit is determined by your preferences:

Spring (April to June): Enjoy great weather, blooming flowers, and less tourists than during the high summer months.

Summer (July-August): This is the peak tourist season, with pleasant temperatures ideal for beach excursions. Popular tourist locations, on the other hand, might become rather crowded.

Autumn (September to October): The weather stays pleasant, making it an ideal time to explore the region without having to battle with the high summer crowds.

Travelers' Cultural Etiquette And Tips

When visiting Southern France, it is critical to observe local customs and etiquette:

Greetings
In interactions, a simple "Bonjour" (Hello) and "Au revoir" (Goodbye) coupled by a smile can go a long way.

Dining
It is usual to welcome the employees when entering and departing local restaurants. In addition, because dining is considered a social event, take your time enjoying it.

Fashion
Southern France is well-known for its fashion-conscious inhabitants. It is best to dress

neatly and avoid overly casual apparel, especially in cities.

Tips For Creating a Travel Budget

Budgeting for a trip to Southern France is dependent on a variety of things, including lodging options, food preferences, and activities. While it might be an expensive vacation, there are ways to keep your costs under control.

In each chapter and for each region of Southern France mentioned in this traveler's guide, there are concrete insights, tips and approximate price value for each service and things you might want to pay for. Such as:

Accommodation
Instead of expensive hotels, consider staying in guesthouses, hostels, or vacation rentals.

Dining
For low-cost meals, visit local markets, bakeries, and smaller restaurants. A three-course lunch at a mid-priced restaurant can give you a taste of French cuisine without breaking the bank.

Public Transportation

Consider taking advantage of public transit, such as trains and buses, which are well-connected and efficient. When hiring a car, research costs and reserve ahead of time to get the best deals.

General Activities And Attractions
Many attractions, like public squares, historical buildings, and stunning landscapes, are free to enter. Look out for city passes that provide discounts on several attractions.

Basic French Phrases

In this chapter also is a collection of fundamental French phrases that will serve as your foundation for effective communication in everyday situations.

Learning these phrases will not only help you navigate through various scenarios in French-speaking regions but also allow you to connect with locals on a more personal level and enhance your overall great experience in southern France.

We'll cover the interpretation of each phrase, along with a guide on how to pronounce them accurately.

Greetings and Introductions

Bonjour (bohn-zhoor) - Hello
Interpretation: A standard greeting used throughout the day.
Usage: Used as a polite way to say hello to anyone, regardless of the time of day.

Salut (sa-loo) - Hi/Hello
Interpretation: An informal way to greet someone.
Usage: Commonly used among friends and acquaintances.

Comment ça va ? (koh-mahn sah vah) - How are you?
Interpretation: Inquiring about someone's well-being.
Usage: An everyday question, typically accompanied by a friendly smile.

Ça va bien, merci. (sah vah byen, mehr-see) - I'm doing well, thank you.
Interpretation: Responding positively to the question "How are you?"
Usage: Polite and common response to convey that you're feeling good.

Enchanté(e) (ahn-shahn-tey) - Nice to meet you
Interpretation: Expressing pleasure upon meeting someone.
Usage: Typically said when introduced to someone for the first time.

Basic Communications

S'il vous plaît (seel voo pleh) - Please
Interpretation: A polite request for something.
Usage: Essential for demonstrating courtesy when asking for assistance or services.

Merci (mehr-see) - Thank you
Interpretation: Expressing gratitude.
Usage: Commonly used to show appreciation after receiving help or a service.

De rien (duh ryen) - You're welcome
Interpretation: Responding to thanks, indicating that the help was given willingly.
Usage: Polite response to acknowledge someone's gratitude.

Excusez-moi (ehk-skew-zay mwah) - Excuse me

Interpretation: Apologizing for a minor inconvenience or seeking someone's attention.
Usage: Used to politely navigate through crowds, interrupt someone, or apologize.

Asking for Directions

Où est... ? (oo eh) - Where is...?
Interpretation: Seeking directions to a specific location.
Usage: Helpful when trying to find a place, such as a street, restaurant, or restroom.

À gauche (ah gohsh) - To the left
Interpretation: Indicating a leftward direction.
Usage: Useful when following directions or guiding someone.

À droite (ah dwat) - To the right
Interpretation: Indicating a rightward direction.
Usage: Similar to "à gauche," this phrase helps with giving or following directions.

Basic Expressions

Oui (wee) - Yes
Interpretation: Affirmative response.

Usage: Used to answer positively to questions or confirm statements.

Non (noh) - No
Interpretation: Negative response.
Usage: Used to answer negatively or reject statements.

Je ne comprends pas (zhuh nuh kohm-prahn pah) - I don't understand.
Interpretation: Expressing confusion or lack of comprehension.
Usage: Useful when you're having difficulty understanding someone.

Farewells

Au revoir (oh ruh-vwahr) - Goodbye
Interpretation: Formal farewell, wishing someone well.
Usage: Appropriate when leaving a formal gathering or saying goodbye to someone you may not see for a while.

À bientôt (ah byen-toh) - See you soon
Interpretation: Expressing the hope to meet again soon.

Usage: Used when parting ways with someone you expect to see in the near future.

À plus tard (ah plew tahr) - See you later
Interpretation: Informal way of saying goodbye.
Usage: Used among friends and in casual situations when you plan to meet again later.

Mastering these basic French phrases will undoubtedly enhance your ability to communicate effectively and connect with French speakers on various occasions.

Whether you're traveling, socializing, or simply aiming to expand your language skills, these phrases will lay the groundwork for your journey into the French language and culture.

Practicing their pronunciation, understanding their meanings, and integrating them into your interactions will make your experiences in French-speaking environments more enjoyable and meaningful. *A Bien tôt !*

Chapter 2

Marseille's Coastal Splendors And Urban Charms

Marseille, a thriving seaside city in southern France, welcomes visitors with a unique combination of historical charm, bustling urban activity, and spectacular natural beauty.

In this chapter, we will look at the numerous aspects of Marseille that make it a must-see for any traveler.

Marseille offers a rich and diversified experience for every sort of traveler, from the gorgeous Old Port to the adventurous Calanques National Park, from cultural immersion at museums and markets to indulging in a wide culinary scene, and from budget-friendly hostels to deluxe hotels.

Hello And Welcome To Marseille

When you arrive in Marseille, you will be met by the brilliant blue waves of the Mediterranean Sea and a bustling environment that reflects the city's strong nautical heritage.

The bustle of lively cafes, street entertainers, and the perfume of freshly cooked baguettes fill the sun-drenched streets.

The city's diversified population adds to its vibrant character, resulting in a distinctively Marseille-blend of cultures.

Visiting the Old Port and the Le Panier District

Begin your adventure by strolling around the historic Old Port (Vieux-Port), which is home to colorful fishing boats and elegant yachts. The lovely sea breeze and charming promenades make it the ideal location for a leisurely stroll.

You will come across a mix of traditional fish markets, seafood eateries, and boutique boutiques as you explore. Le Panier, Marseille's oldest neighborhood, is located adjacent to the Old Port.

This artsy and bohemian district is a maze of winding streets, lovely squares, and colorful facades. Explore the colourful street art, explore local art galleries, and get lost in Le Panier's enchanting ambiance.

Adventure in the Calanques National Park

Calanques National Park offers a haven of natural beauty just a short distance from the city for nature enthusiasts and adventure seekers.

The park is known for its breathtaking limestone cliffs, secret coves, and crystal-clear waters. Hiking routes wind through the terrain, leading to stunning views of the Mediterranean.

This natural beauty provides a memorable experience whether you are trekking, rock climbing, or simply swimming in the turquoise waters of the calanques.

Museums and markets

provides opportunities for cultural immersion
In its museums and marketplaces, Marseille's rich history and cultural diversity are on full show.

The Museum of European and Mediterranean Civilizations *(MuCEM)* is a symbol of Marseille's nautical past and investigates cultural linkages.

The lively Noailles Market is a sensory overload of colors, scents, and sensations that highlights the city's varied food scene. Dive into the market's bustling lanes to find a diverse selection of spices, fresh food, and regional delicacies.

Where to Eat and Drink

From Cheap to Gourmet
The gastronomic scene in Marseille is a voyage in and of itself, catering to all tastes and budgets. At local bistros or luxury restaurants, try a typical bouillabaisse, a savory fish stew that originated in Marseille.

As you tour the city's many neighborhoods, savor freshly caught fish, artisan cheeses, and Provencal delicacies. Do not miss out on a drink of pastis, the renowned anise-flavored apéritif, at a beautiful café while watching the world go by for a true sense of Marseille.

Options for lodging

Range from hostels to luxury hotels.
Marseille has a variety of lodging alternatives to suit every traveler's needs. Budget-conscious travelers can discover nice and reasonable hostels in the city center, allowing them to meet other travelers.

Waterfront hotels provide spectacular views of the Mediterranean as well as relaxing amenities for those seeking a touch of luxury.

Alternatively, stay in boutique guesthouses dotted across Marseille's neighborhoods to immerse yourself in the city's artistic vibe.

Marseille 3 Days Itinerary

Here is a three days itinerary for going to Marseille and having a thorough complete pleasure-full time:

Day 1

Visiting the Old Port and the Le Panier District
- Begin your adventure by wandering through the spectacular Vieux-Port (Old Port), which has fishing boats and yachts against a backdrop of antique buildings.

- For roughly €5, pick up a freshly baked croissant and a coffee from a local bakery and enjoy your breakfast while watching the waterfront come alive with activity.

- After that, make your way to Marseille's oldest neighborhood, Le Panier. Explore small lanes with colorful facades, artisan boutiques, and delightful cafés.

- Visit the Vieille Charité, a historic site that currently houses museums and exhibitions (admission fee: approximately €6).

- For lunch, a superb bowl of bouillabaisse, a traditional fish stew, may be had for roughly €20 at a local café.

Day 2

Calanques National Park Adventure
- On day 2, Visit Calanques National Park, a natural beauty of jagged limestone cliffs, crystal-clear lakes, and secret coves, for a memorable day excursion.

- A guided hiking tour, which includes transportation, costs around €40. Alternatively, for roughly €30, rent a kayak and paddle over the turquoise seas to discover secret beaches and stunning views.

- Pack a picnic for the day or stop by a local deli for a sandwich for roughly €8. Remember to bring plenty of water and sunscreen with you because the sun may be fairly harsh.

Day 3

Museums and Markets for Cultural Immersion
- Visit the museums in Marseille to immerse yourself in the city's rich culture. The MuCEM (Museum of European and Mediterranean Civilisations) provides information about the region's history and heritage (admission fee: approximately €9).

- The Musée des Beaux-Arts has an amazing collection of paintings and sculptures for art lovers (admission fee: roughly €8).

- Explore the lively marketplaces of the afternoon, such as the Marché de la Joliette or the Marché de la Plaine.

- Enjoy fresh produce, cheeses, olives, and other regional specialties. Set aside about €15 for a market haul to make a tasty picnic meal.

Where to Eat and Drink

From Cheap to Gourmet
- The dining scene in Marseille caters to a wide range of preferences and budgets. Grab a fantastic falafel wrap from a street vendor for roughly €6 for an economical yet authentic experience.

- If you are seeking a gourmet treat, try Le Petit Nice Passedat, a Michelin-starred restaurant where a multi-course meal can cost around €150 per person.

Accommodation Options in Marseilles
- Marseille has a wide range of housing options, from hostels to luxury hotels. Dormitory beds at hostels can be had for

around €20-€40 per night for budget tourists.

- Mid-range options, such as boutique hotels or guesthouses, might cost between €80 and €150 per night. For €200 and above, luxury seekers can enjoy sumptuous comfort in 5-star hotels.

Chapter 3

Nice Riviera Elegance And Mediterranean Bliss

The city of Nice, like a rare gem on the picturesque French Riviera, exerts an irresistible spell on everyone who strolls its charming streets and in its dazzling Mediterranean warmth.

This chapter reveals the enthralling essence of Nice, transporting you to a world where Riviera attractiveness, historical grandeur, cultural richness, and the gentle embrace of the Mediterranean meets, in harmonic glory.

The French-Riviera's Allure

The French Riviera, often known as the Côte d'Azur, has long captivated the imaginations of painters, writers, and jetsetters.

Its charm is a seductive blend of sumptuous grandeur, natural beauty, and a relaxed grace that lingers in the air.

The Riviera's exquisite beauty has served as a muse for innumerable creative minds, its azure waters and scenic landscapes immortalized in both canvas and text, with Nice as its incandescent centerpiece.

Cultural Diversity and Historical Importance

Aside from its natural beauty, Nice has a long history dating back millennia. Traces of its history can be seen in the Old Town's cobblestone streets, where each weathered stone tells a story of ancient civilizations, Roman conquests, and maritime influences.

This city has always been a cultural crossroads, a meeting place for French, Italian, and Mediterranean identities.

From the colorful markets to the diverse cuisine, this cultural tapestry is woven into the fabric of everyday life, reflecting a harmonious fusion of traditions and lifestyles.

The Mediterranean Climate and Its Implications

Nice enjoys a climate that is nothing short of beautiful, thanks to the gentle caress of the Mediterranean Sea. The pleasant sun-kissed days and temperate evenings create an appealing atmosphere.

The presence of the Mediterranean brings vitality to every part of the city, from the vivid hues of the sea and the azure skies to the verdant landscapes that thrive under its benign touch.

This climate has influenced not just the physical landscape but also the rhythms of life, influencing the outdoor cafes, leisurely promenades, and bustling street scenes that characterize Nice.

Nice' 3 Days Itinerary

Allow the attraction of the French Riviera, the tapestry of history and culture, and the relaxing embrace of the Mediterranean environment to enchant your senses and call you to immerse yourself in the various activities that await as we travel further into the heart of Nice using these 3 days itinerary plan.

Day One
Promenade des Anglais and Old Town Exploration

Begin your journey down the world-famous Promenade des Anglais, a coastal promenade that captures the soul of Nice. As you meander by turquoise waters, palm-fringed pathways, and colorful street entertainers, feel the calm sea wind.

Explore the Old Town's beautiful maze, where centuries-old buildings bear testament to the city's rich history. Enjoy the sights and smells of fresh food, flowers, and local crafts at the Cours Saleya market.

Enjoy a slice of Socca, a traditional Niçoise dish, while you are there. Its crispy outside and delicate inside provide a delectable flavor of the region.

- Stroll along the iconic Promenade des Anglais
- Beaches, palm trees, and vibrant street life
- Explore the charming Old Town (Vieux Nice)
- Cours Saleya market and its fresh produce
- Sample Socca, a local chickpea pancake

- Approximate cost: Free (promenade), €5-10 (Socca)

Day Two

Chagall and Matisse: Artistic Treasures

Explore Nice's artistic legacy through the eyes of Marc Chagall and Henri Matisse. The Marc Chagall National Museum exhibits the artist's bright and dreamy works, allowing visitors to become immersed in the artist's imagination.

In contrast, Henri Matisse's former home has been turned into a museum honoring his groundbreaking contributions to contemporary art. Explore the progression of their styles through interactive exhibits and informative audio guides.

- Marc Chagall National Museum showcasing modernist art
- Henri Matisse's former residence, now a museum
- Dive into the evolution of their art styles
- Engaging audio guides and interactive exhibits
- Approximate cost: €10-15 per museum

Day Three

Visit Ze Village and Monaco

Set out on an adventure outside Nice's bounds. Ascend to Ze, a hilltop medieval village with cobblestone lanes that twist through lovely alleys.

The Exotic Garden rewards your ascent with breathtaking views of the turquoise shoreline. Continue your journey to Monaco, the sumptuous principality that serves as a playground for the wealthy and famous.

Admire the splendor of the Monte Carlo Casino, a work of art in terms of opulence and architectural design. The Changing of the Guard at the Prince's Palace is a timeless event that provides an insight into the region's historical heritage.

- Visit Èze, a picturesque hilltop village
- Cobblestone streets, stunning views, and boutiques
- Exotic garden offering panoramic vistas
- Proceed to the luxurious principality of Monaco
- Explore the opulent Monte Carlo Casino

- Witness the Changing of the Guard at the Prince's Palace
- Approximate cost: €5-10 (Èze garden), €17 (Monte Carlo Casino entrance)

Delights in Dining

From Niçoise Cuisine to International Flavors
Experience the essence of Niçoise food, a delectable blend of Mediterranean tastes. Salade Niçoise is a colorful medley of fresh vegetables, olives, anchovies, and tuna.

Ratatouille, a vegetable stew that symbolizes the region's agricultural abundance, is a savory delight. Socca, a scrumptious chickpea pancake that reflects the passion of Nice's street food culture, will tantalize your taste buds.

Local varieties, such as Bellet AOC, are an ideal compliment to your gastronomic trip for wine connoisseurs. If you are looking for a variety of culinary experiences, Nice has foreign eateries to suit every taste.

- Experience authentic Niçoise cuisine
- Salade Niçoise with fresh local ingredients

- Socca, Ratatouille, and Pissaladière
- Try local wines like Bellet AOC
- International restaurants catering to diverse palates
- Approximate cost: €15-30 (meal), €5-10 (glass of wine)

Budget Inns to Seaside Resorts for Rest and Rejuvenation

The city's accommodations range from modest budget inns tucked in the heart of Vieux Nice, ideal for the economical traveler seeking local authenticity, to mid-range boutique hotels radiating Niçoise charm.

Choosing a place to stay is an important element of your Nice experience. Indulge in the luxury of seaside resorts with panoramic views of the Mediterranean horizon for those seeking ultimate relaxation.

Recharge your batteries with spa treatments that combine the calming force of the water with current wellness practices.

- Diverse range of accommodation options
- Cozy budget inns in Vieux Nice
- Mid-range boutique hotels with local charm

- Seaside resorts offering luxurious amenities
- Unwind at a spa overlooking the Mediterranean
- Approximate cost: €50-100 (budget inn), €100-200 (boutique hotel), varies for resorts

Chapter 4

Avignon - Papal History and Provençal Delights

Avignon, a charming city in France's Provence region, has a rich history entwined with papal heritage and a tapestry of Provençal charms.

This chapter takes you on an enthralling tour of Avignon's attractions, from the awe-inspiring Palais des Papes to the famed Pont Saint-Bénézet.

You will see the lovely Luberon villages of Gordes and Roussillon, as well as go on a gourmet tour through traditional Provençal cuisine.

Relax in Avignon's boutique hotels and riverside hotels, which capture the soul of this wonderful city, to round out your experience.

Discovering Avignon's Allure

As soon as you foot into Avignon, you are taken to a world of medieval charm and architectural marvels. The **Palais des Papes** *(Palace of the Popes),* the city's most recognizable structure, stands proudly as a tribute to Avignon's role as the seat of the pope in the 14th century.

This enormous fortress-like palace, designated as a UNESCO World Heritage site, features exquisite Gothic architecture and huge hallways that resound with whispers of past papal authority.

The famous Pont Saint-Bénézet, popularly known as the Pont d'Avignon, lies just next to the palace. This old bridge, immortalized in the traditional song "Sur le Pont d'Avignon," spans the Rhône River in part. Its graceful arches and rich history convey a sense of timelessness, prompting visitors to contemplate on years gone by.

Exploring Luberon Villages

Gordes and Roussillon

While Avignon itself is a historical treasure trove, the surrounding countryside has its own set of attractions. A short journey from Avignon takes you to the lovely Luberon towns, where time appears to stand still.

Gordes, perched atop a rocky slope, provides sweeping views of the surrounding countryside. Its cobblestone pathways lead via winding alleyways to secret squares filled with fountains and bright bougainvillea.

Roussillon, often known as the "Ochre Village," is a colorful kaleidoscope. The buildings in the village are painted in various colors of red and orange, matching nicely with the natural ochre cliffs that surround it.

A visit through Roussillon is like strolling through an artist's palette, a living witness to the region's distinctive geology.

Traditional Provençal Flavors

on a Culinary Journey

A trip to Avignon would be incomplete without sampling the delights of Provençal food. The brilliant hues and fragrances of fresh vegetables, cheeses, meats, and local delicacies fill the city's marketplaces, such as Les Halles.

Try the fragrant herbs of the region, such as thyme, rosemary, and lavender, which add a particular flavor to Provençal meals. Enjoy ratatouille, a variety of perfectly prepared vegetables, or delve into a bowl of bouillabaisse, a substantial fish stew that captures the essence of coastal living.

Do not pass up the chance to sample the rich tastes of olive tapenade, locally-cured olives, and artisanal cheeses, which match nicely with a bottle of regional wine.

Avignon Relaxation

Boutique Hotels and Riverside Hotels
Retire to the luxury of Avignon's boutique stays and riverside hotels after a day of discovery and culinary indulgence. These apartments elegantly integrate modern luxury with the historical setting of the city.

Imagine waking up to views of the Palais des Papes from your window, or enjoying wine on a patio overlooking the peaceful Rhône River. Avignon has much to offer everyone, from lovely bed and breakfasts to exquisite boutique hotels.

The great welcome of the city ensures that your stay is more than just a place to stay, but also a continuation of the immersive experience that Avignon has to offer.

3 Days Itinerary For Avignon

Discovering Avignon's Allure

Day 1
- Papes Palace and Pont Saint-Bénézet
- A Glimpse of Papal History at the Palais des Papes
- A visit to the Palais des Papes, a vast medieval palace that served as the residence for successive popes, will transport you to the heart of Avignon's history.
- Explore sumptuous apartments, breathtaking churches, and breathtaking murals depicting the papal heritage.
- Experience an audio-guided tour that gives detailed commentary on the palace's history and significance.

Price approximation: The entry fee is €12.

Crossing the Saint-Bénézet Pont
- Wander along the Rhône River and admire the Pont Saint-Bénézet, also known as the "Pont d'Avignon."
- Learn about the bridge's intriguing history, which goes back to the 12th century and formerly crossed the river.

- Enjoy stunning views of the Avignon skyline and neighboring surroundings.
- Consider taking a guided tour to learn more about the bridge's history and progress.

Price approximation: €8 for a guided tour

Day 2
Visit Luberon villages Gordes and Roussillon

Gordes: A Hilltop Treasure

- Take a picturesque journey to Gordes, a charming hilltop village known for its stone homes and medieval beauty.
- Explore the Luberon Valley's small lanes, explore artisan boutiques, and take in the panoramic views.
- Visit the Gordes Castle and Gardens, which combine history and natural beauty in an amazing way.
- Discover the local market, where you can buy homemade products, fresh fruit, and souvenirs.

Price approximation: Castle admission - €10 2.2 Ochre-Hued Delights in Roussillon

- Continue your journey to Roussillon, which is known for its distinctive ochre cliffs and colorful environment.
- Explore the "Sentier des Ocres," a trail that goes through the vibrant ochre formations and provides a breathtaking visual display.
- Explore the region's artistic heritage by visiting local art galleries and studios.
- Indulge in a leisurely supper at a quaint Provençal café, savoring cuisine made from fresh ingredients found locally.

Price approximation: Trail admission is €5, and a café dinner is €25.

Traditional Provençal Flavors on a Culinary Journey

A Flavorful Feast

- A guided food tour through Avignon's bustling markets and small cafés will immerse you in the Provençal gastronomic scene.
- Try ratatouille, bouillabaisse, tapenade, and lavender-infused sweets, among other regional specialties.
- Interact with dedicated chefs and artisans who will reveal the secrets to creating these traditional meals.

- Consider taking a cooking class to learn how to make these Provençal flavors at home.

Price approximation: €50 for a food tour, €80 for a cooking class

Avignon Relaxation
Boutique Hotels and Riverside Hotels

Adorable Boutique Hotels
- Retire to a delightful boutique hotel that embodies Avignon's historic and cultural environment.
- Enjoy individualized service, comfortable rooms, and distinctive design elements that represent the region's history.
- Relax in secluded courtyards or rooftop terraces, immersed in the peaceful ambiance of Provence.

Price approximation: €120 for a one-night stay in a boutique hotel.

The Riverside Elegance
- Choose a riverfront hotel overlooking the Rhône that offers spectacular views and a tranquil location to indulge in luxury.
- Relax in chic rooms with exquisite furniture and modern facilities.

- Enjoy gourmet meals at the hotel's restaurant, where you can sample a fusion of Provençal and foreign cuisines.
- Enjoy a leisurely stroll along the riverbanks while taking in the scenery.

Price approximation: Hotel stay in Riverside (per night) - €200

You will be intrigued by the rich amount of experiences this fascinating city has to offer as you discover Avignon's papal heritage, picturesque countryside, and wonderful cuisine. Avignon promises a journey of discovery that will leave you with cherished recollections of your time in the heart of Provence, from architectural marvels to culinary delights.

Chapter 5

Montpellier - Modern Energy and Medieval Roots

Montpellier Unveiled

Montpellier, a charming city in southern France, seamlessly blends modern vigor with its historic heritage.

This chapter digs into Montpellier's strong cultural scene, architectural marvels, and culinary delights, which make it a must-see destination.

Historic Streets and Eclectic Architecture

Montpellier has an architectural tapestry that conveys the tale of its vivid history and rich past.

The small cobblestone alleyways, hidden courtyards, and majestic cathedrals that decorate the city reflect the city's medieval roots.

With its neoclassical opera house and lively modern cafes, Montpellier's renowned Place de la Comédie represents the city's mix of old and new.

Wandering around the ancient neighborhood, travelers will come upon the majestic Saint Pierre Cathedral, a Gothic masterpiece that has stood for centuries.

The Porte du Peyrou, an archway that leads to the Promenade du Peyrou, provides stunning views of the city and surrounding countryside.

Languedoc Wine Tasting and Local Cuisine

A trip to Montpellier would be incomplete without sampling the region's world-renowned wines. The Languedoc region is a wine lover's dream, and Montpellier is the ideal starting point for exploring its vineyards.

Join a guided wine tour to learn the secrets of producing strong reds, crisp whites, and exquisite rosés. Sample the wines where they are made and obtain an understanding of the artistry that goes into each bottle.

Immerse yourself in Montpellier's local gastronomy after a day of exploration. Traditional meals include "petit pâté de Pézenas" (a savory pie), "tielle sétoise" (a seafood-filled pastry), and "brandade de morue" (salt cod puree).

You can also relax in a beautiful café hidden away in a medieval alley, where the ambience is as delicious as the food.

La Grande Motte Beach Escape

Take a short drive from Montpellier to the sun-drenched sanctuary of La Grande Motte for a change of scenery. This sophisticated seaside resort provides a quiet getaway from the city's busy streets.

Dip your toes in the golden sands, cool yourself in the Mediterranean Sea, or participate in a range of water sports and activities.

The avant-garde architecture of La Grande Motte, with its pyramid-shaped buildings, provides a touch of modernism to the seaside scene.

Accommodation for Everyone

From Student-Friendly to Upscale Options

Montpellier welcomes all types of visitors with a varied choice of lodging alternatives.

Budget-conscious backpackers will find comfort at hostels located in the city's core, providing convenient access to the city's exciting nightlife and cultural attractions.

Upscale hotels provide magnificent accommodations, wellness amenities, and stunning views of Montpellier's skyline for visitors wanting a touch of luxury.

Montpellier attracts students because of its outstanding universities, and the city meets their demands by providing affordable student housing.

These lodgings offer a one-of-a-kind opportunity to become immersed in the local student population and experience the city's youthful vibe.

Montpellier Itinerary

The First Day

Eclectic Architecture and Historic Streets

Morning
- Begin your day at Place de la Comédie, the city's heart, which is noted for its beautiful opera theater and lively ambiance. Admire the magnificent 19th-century architecture.

- Explore Écusson's historic district, which is distinguished by its small medieval alleys and lovely squares.

- Visit the Saint-Pierre Cathedral, a blend of Gothic and Romanesque styles that reflects the city's rich past.

Lunch

- Lunch at Le Petit Jardin, a charming restaurant with a fusion of French and Mediterranean food. Prices range from €15 to €30 per person.

Afternoon

- Discover the one-of-a-kind Antigone District, built by Ricardo Bofill and displaying contemporary neoclassical architecture.

- Take a trip down the Peyrou Promenade, which has the historic Saint-Clément Aqueduct and the Montpellier Arc de Triomphe.

Dinner

- Enjoy a sumptuous evening at La Diligence, a Michelin-starred restaurant specializing in inventive French cuisine. The cost per person is between €50 and €100.

Day 2
Wine Tasting and Local Gastronomy in Languedoc

Morning

- Take a guided tour of the ancient wine estate Château de Flaugergues. Learn about the surrounding vineyards and partake in wine tastings. The tour costs between €20 and €30 per person.

- Discover Les Halles Castellane, a lively indoor market filled with fresh local goods.

Lunch

- Enjoy a relaxed lunch at Le Marché du Lez, an open-air market with food trucks and kiosks offering a variety of gastronomic options. Prices range from €10 to €20 per person.

Afternoon

- Visit the Musée Fabre, which houses a large collection of European art from the 15th to the 19th centuries.

- Take a stroll along the Promenade du Peyrou, which offers panoramic views of the city.

Dinner

- Leclere & Fils serves authentic Languedoc cuisine. Cassoulet and seafood bouillabaisse are popular meals. Prices range from €25 to €40 per person.

Day 3
La Grande Motte Beach Escape

Morning

- Visit La Grande Motte, a nearby coastal town famed for its modern architecture and stunning beaches, for a day excursion.

- Relax on the beach, swim in the Mediterranean Sea, or participate in water sports.

Lunch
- La Plage des Artistes serves fresh seafood and Mediterranean delicacies for a beachside lunch. Prices range from €20 to €35 per person.

Afternoon
- Discover the one-of-a-kind architecture of La Grande Motte, constructed by architect Jean Balladur, with its characteristic pyramidal structures.

- Enjoy the coastal ambience while strolling along the marina.

Dinner
- Return to Montpellier and lunch at La Réserve Rimbaud, a quaint restaurant with a view of the Lez River. Prices range from €30 to €50 per person.

Accommodation for Everyone
from student-friendly to upscale

- Hostels with dormitory-style rooms, such as Hostel Montpellier and Sunflower Hostel, are ideal for budget tourists. Prices range from €20 to €40 per night.

- Hotel ibis Montpellier Centre and Hotel Oceania Le Métropole are mid-range options with decent accommodations and convenient locations. The price range is €70-120 per night.

- Consider Domaine de Verchant and Pullman Montpellier Centre for a magnificent stay with upscale amenities and outstanding service. Prices range from €150 to €300+ each night.

This chapter delves into Montpellier's many sides, from its architectural wonders and historical charm to its fine cuisine and lodging options, making it a well-rounded and unforgettable travel experience.

Chapter 6

Aix-en Provence - Art, Culture, and Sophistication

Aix-en-Provence, located in the scenic region of Provence in southern France, is a city that seamlessly combines history, art, culture, and luxury.

Aix-en-Provence has long drawn visitors seeking a mix of relaxation and cultural inquiry, thanks to its tree-lined avenues, beautiful squares, and rich artistic past.

In this chapter, we will explore Aix-en-Provence's center, discovering its artistic treasures, colorful marketplaces, culinary delights, and luxurious hotels.

Introducing Aix-en-Provence

As soon as you step foot in Aix-en-Provence, you will be enchanted by its unmistakable charm and refinement. The city's unique blend of Provençal architecture, Roman influences, and medieval history produces an enticing ambiance that is impossible to resist.

The city's cobblestone lanes wind through it, revealing hidden courtyards, antique fountains, and gorgeous facades that take you back in time.

Cours Mirabeau and Museums Galore

Aix-en-Provence is an art lover's paradise, with a plethora of museums and galleries. Begin your cultural exploration with a stroll down the renowned Cours Mirabeau, an avenue studded with gigantic plane trees and exquisite houses.

You will be surrounded by elegant boutiques, attractive cafés, and a dynamic street life that embodies the city's personality as you walk down this lively boulevard.

The Musée Granet is a must-see for art lovers. This museum has an outstanding collection of European paintings, sculptures, and decorative arts spanning the 16th to the 20th century.

The Musée Granet offers a wide and intriguing exploration of artistic expression, ranging from Old Masters to modern works.

Exploring Local Markets and Cézanne's Trails

Explore Aix's vibrant markets to immerse yourself in the local culture. Place Richelme's market is a sensory feast, with stalls brimming with fresh food, aromatic herbs, and regional specialties.

Interact with local sellers, try artisanal cheeses, and enjoy the brilliant colors and flavors that define Provençal cuisine.

The city of Aix-en-Provence is inextricably tied to the famous artist Paul Cézanne, who found unending inspiration in the area's surroundings.

Travel in Cézanne's footsteps by following the Cézanne Trail, which brings you to the locations that inspired his classic paintings.

You can also explore the Montagne Sainte-Victoire, the Bibémus Quarries, and other picturesque locales that influenced Cézanne's aesthetic vision.

A Gourmet Escape Through Aix's Culinary Scene

Aix's booming culinary scene combines classic Provençal delicacies with modern gastronomy. The city's restaurants range from tiny bistros to Michelin-starred establishments, each providing a distinct gastronomic experience.

Dishes such as bouillabaisse, ratatouille, and lavender-infused sweets pay respect to the region's abundant resources. The Le Grand Marché, located in the center of Aix-en-Provence, offers an unparalleled gastronomy experience.

This premium market offers a carefully curated variety of local ingredients from which to make your own Provençal feast. Engage in discussions with passionate food artisans, and let their knowledge lead you in choosing the best cheeses, wines, and olive oils.

Where To Stay

Elegant Hotels and Charming Inns

Relax in one of Aix-en-Provence's beautiful inns or exquisite hotels to round out your visit. This city's accommodations are meant to enhance your experience by combining comfort, luxury, and authenticity.

The old luxury hotel Le Pigonnet exudes refinement.
Set in a verdant garden, this magnificent house provides a tranquil haven just minutes from the city center. Enjoy exceptional service, exquisite décor, and a sense of tranquillity that complements your tour of Aix-en-Provence.

La Maison d'Aix
Consider La Maison d'Aix, a boutique hotel that embraces the character of the city, for a more personal environment. La Maison d'Aix is a haven of relaxation and style, with precisely crafted suites, a spa, and a stunning courtyard.

Itinerary for Aix-en-Provence

Day 1
The Cours Mirabeau and Museums Abound

Morning
Start your exploration of Aix-en-Provence with a stroll down the famous Cours Mirabeau. This sophisticated promenade is lined with centuries-old plane trees, attractive cafes, and boutique shops.

Grab a croissant and a café au lait from a nearby bakery to savor while taking in the sights and sounds of the busy street.

Afternoon

Visit Aix's renowned museums to immerse yourself in the city's vibrant cultural landscape. The Musée Granet is a treasure trove of European art, including paintings by Picasso, Van Gogh, and Rembrandt on display. Admission is around €10.

The Musée du Vieil Aix, housed in a 17th-century mansion, provides an insight into the town's past. It provides insight into the town's evolution over time. Admission is approximately €6.

Evening

As the day comes to a close, indulge yourself to a gourmet meal at one of Aix's luxury restaurants.
The sophisticated Provençal cuisine with a modern flair at Le Formal is well-known. Indulge in recipes like bouillabaisse or crème brûlée with lavender. Prices range from €50 to €80 per person.

Day 2
Local Markets and Trails of Cézanne
Morning

Take a stroll through Aix's bustling local markets. The Marché d'Aix-en-Provence is a sensory overload, with fresh fruit, cheeses, olives, and handcrafted goods. Engage with local sellers and collect ingredients for a later picnic.

Afternoon

Explore Aix's artistic past by following along the footsteps of great painter Paul Cézanne. Explore the artist's personal connection with the settings that inspired his works at the Atelier Cézanne, his old studio. Admission is approximately €8.

Continue your Cézanne journey by visiting Montagne Sainte-Victoire, a spectacular peak that appears in several of his paintings. Enjoy a trek or a leisurely drive around the mountain to take in the breathtaking views that captured the artist's mind.

Evening

Create your own Provencal-inspired picnic using the market findings from the morning and enjoy it in a lovely location such as the Parc Jourdan. Enjoy local cheeses, baguettes, and fruits while basking in the golden colors of the setting sun.

A Gourmet Escape Through Aix's Culinary Scene

Enjoy a wine and cheese tasting at a nearby cellar or a typical Provençal supper at La Table du Comtadin. Prices range from €20 to €100 or more per person depending on the experience.

Where to Stay
Elegant Hotels and Charming Inns
Consider the charming Hotel Le Pigonnet for an enjoyable stay. This 18th-century country mansion is surrounded by magnificent grounds and provides a blend of luxury and history.
Prices start at around €150 per night.

Alternatively, the beautiful Grand Hôtel Roi René Aix-en-Provence Centre is centrally located and equipped with modern conveniences. The nightly rate begins at about €120.

Aix-en-Provence has a variety of hotels to fit your interests and budget, whether you select a historical inn or a modern hotel.

As you immerse yourself in Aix's art, culture, and refinement, you will discover that every corner of this town has a tale to tell. Aix-en-Provence delivers a trip of richness and enchantment, from its lively streets to its tranquil countryside.

Chapter 7

Arles's Ancient Heritage and Van Gogh's Legacy

Arles, a lovely town in southern France, is a paradise for history buffs, art connoisseurs, and environment lovers alike. This chapter will delve into the enthralling attractions and activities that make Arles a must-see location.

Arles offers a unique blend of cultural experiences that transport visitors through time and artistic brilliance, thanks to its rich Roman heritage and close ties to the great artist Vincent van Gogh.

Roman Ruins and Van Gogh Walking Tour in Arles

Arles is a living testimony to its Roman past, with cobblestone streets and exquisite architecture telling the story. With its towering walls and layers of seating, the Roman Amphitheatre, an iconic monument, conjures the grandeur of ancient spectacles.

The Roman Theatre, located nearby, serves as a reminder of the artistic inclinations of the time, providing a glimpse into the culture and amusement of yesteryears.

- The Arena (Amphitheatre): Immerse yourself in the splendor of a historic amphitheater where gladiator fights once captivated audiences. (Estimated entry fee: €10)

No trip to Arles is complete unless you immerse yourself in the world of Vincent Van Gogh. The town inspired some of his most famous works, and a Van Gogh Walking Tour takes visitors to the locations that inspired his masterpieces.

The Yellow House and the Café Terrace at Night come to life, resonating with the artist's impassioned brushstrokes and profound feelings.

- You can Visit Van Gogh's former hospital and marvel at the site that inspired some of his works. (Average entry fee: €9)

- Discover the real-life setting that inspired one of Van Gogh's renowned paintings, Café Terrace at Night.

Exploration of the Camargue and Wildlife Encounters

Beyond Arles, the vastness of the Camargue region beckons. This one-of-a-kind wetland is teeming with varied habitats, ranging from salt marshes to lagoons, and serves as a haven for a variety of creatures.

Flamingos wade in the shallow waters, their vivid colors reflecting the sunset, while white horses gallop through the vast countryside, signifying freedom.

A Camargue Exploration allows you to view these spectacular vistas firsthand. Guided excursions allow tourists to view the delicate balance of the environment and learn about the traditions of local ranchers who have fostered a happy coexistence with nature for decades.

From Bistros to Riverside Cafés, Dining on the Rhône

Arles' culinary culture is a celebration of Provençal flavors, where dining is transformed into a sensory experience. Bistros hidden away in winding lanes serve meals loaded with the finest local ingredients, combined with superb wines that capture the soul of the region.

The perfume of Provence herbs wafts from kitchens, enticing pedestrians to sample the region's gastronomic riches. The Rhône's riverside cafés provide an ideal environment for a leisurely dinner.

As the sun sets below the horizon, leaving a golden glow on the lake, diners enjoy bouillabaisse, ratatouille, and other regional delights, relaxing to the calm beat of the river.

Finding Rest In Cozy Guest Houses And Historic Inns

The accommodations in Arles are a beautiful blend of old-world charm and modern conveniences. There is something for everyone, from charming guest houses decked with vivid flowers to historic inns with stories to share.

Traveling into these establishments is like traveling back in time, as the architecture and design tell stories of bygone eras.

Consider staying at a historic hotel that has kept its own character while providing modern conveniences for a fully immersive experience.

These lodgings provide not only a place to stay but also an opportunity to become a part of the town's history and its wholesome traditions. *(itinerary for accommodation is at the end of the chapter)*

2 Days Itinerary for Arles

Day 1
Roman Ruins and Walking Tour of Van Gogh

Morning
- *Discover Roman history:* Begin your day by visiting the majestic Amphitheatre and imagining the shows that once took place within its walls.

- *Visit the Antique Theatre:* From this well-preserved Roman theater, you can enjoy beautiful views of Arles. (Average entry fee: €9)

Van Gogh Walking Tour in the Afternoon
- Follow in Van Gogh's footsteps by visiting the locations that influenced his paintings, such as the Langlois Bridge and the Yellow House.

Day 2
Wildlife Encounters and Camargue Exploration

Morning
- Explore the Camargue: Take a guided tour of the Camargue region, which is known for its spectacular landscapes, salt flats, and wild horses.

- Visit the Parc Ornithologique du Pont de Gau to see a wide variety of bird species in their natural environment. (Average admission fee: €7)

Wildlife Adventures For The Afternoon

- Join a horseback riding expedition to get a close look at the famous Camargue horses. (Approximate price: €50)

- Discover the splendor of this vast lagoon and its resident flamingos at the Étang de Vaccarès.

Rhône Dining
From Bistros to Riverside Cafés

Culinary Delights in Le Galoubet
- This quaint cafe recognized for its local products and friendly environment serves Provençal cuisine. (A lunch costs approximately €30.)

- La Gueule du Loup: Enjoy riverfront dining with a delightful range of seafood and traditional French meals at La Gueule du Loup. (A lunch costs approximately €40.)

Finding Rest In Cozy Guest Houses And Historic Inns
- Le Cloître: Enjoy luxury in a former 12th-century monastery, complete with attractively constructed apartments and a

peaceful courtyard. (Approximate nightly rate: €180)

- Hôtel du Musée: Immerse yourself in history at this hotel, which is decorated with local art and provides excellent lodging. (Approximate nightly rate: €120)

Arles' rich tapestry of history and art entices visitors to discover its riches. The town offers an extraordinary voyage through time and artistic expression, from ancient ruins to bright landscapes that once inspired Van Gogh's masterpieces.

Whether you are charmed by its Roman past or the attraction of its modern-day beauty, Arles will leave an everlasting impact on your heart and spirit!

Chapter 8

Nimes, The Roman Grandeur And Southern Charisma

Nimes Fascinates!

Nimes, located in the heart of the enchanting region of Provence, is a city where Roman history and Southern French charm coexist peacefully. As you walk through its cobblestone streets and vivid squares, you will be intrigued by Nimes' rich history and the bustling ambiance that surrounds the city.

Nimes provides a genuinely unique blend of grandeur and personality, from its well-preserved Roman remains to its vibrant local markets. Steeped in history dating back to the Roman era, has an enigmatic allure that draws travelers from all over the world.

As you walk through the city's small streets, you will discover hidden corners embellished with ancient landmarks and modern surprises.

Venture into the heart of Nimes, where the Amphitheatre, a testimony to the city's past greatness, takes center stage. Imagine the roars of the people as gladiators once battled within its towering walls, a spectacle that has endured throughout history.

Amphitheatre and Maison Carrée
...Time Stops Here
The Amphitheatre is an architectural marvel that transports you back to the days of Roman performances. Imagine the grandeur of events that occurred here centuries ago as you foot atop its aged stones.

The Amphitheatre still hosts cultural performances today, giving new life to its old stones. The nearby Maison Carrée is a beautiful relic of Roman workmanship, its ornate façade a monument to the past's architectural prowess.

Jardins de la Fontaine and Local Markets
For A Peaceful Retreat

Get away from the hustle and bustle of the city and relax in the serene embrace of Jardins de la Fontaine. Amidst finely planted gardens, elaborate fountains, and covered promenades, this lush haven invites reflection.

The Roman Temple of Diana adorns the gardens, lending a mysterious aura to the setting. Explore Nimes' lively culture by meandering around its local markets, where the colors, fragrances, and sounds of Provence come to life.

Here also, you can engage with local artisans, enjoy regional delicacies, and purchase one-of-a-kind gifts that exemplify the spirit of the South.

Nîmoise Delicacies And Culinary Temptations

No trip to Nimes is complete without sampling the local cuisine, and this Chapter delves into the world of Nîmoise delights, tantalizing your taste buds with a delicious symphony.

From the famed Brandade de Nîmes to the exquisite Picholine olives, indulge in hearty dishes that embody the essence of Provençal cuisine.

Discover the art of mixing wines with local fare, a talent passed down through generations, and immerse yourself in the gastronomic delights of Nimes.

Accommodation Options

Charming B&Bs And Modern Hotels
Nimes offers a broad choice of accommodations to suit every traveler's preference, whether you seek a lovely getaway or sophisticated luxury.

There's a variety of options, including intimate and lovely bed and breakfasts that emanate a sense of home away from home, as well as sleek and stylish contemporary hotels that pamper you with every comfort.

Nimes invites you to rest and revitalize in style, with its combination of ancient ambiance and modern comforts.

Nimes Itinerary

Day 1
At The Amphitheatre And Maison Carrée

The Arena With A Sneak Peek Into Ancient Spectacles

- Discover the Roman Empire's magnificence in the Nimes Arena, an exceptionally preserved amphitheatre.
- Investigate the massive structure where gladiators once clashed and people cheered.
- Discover historical echoes in the stands and corridors.

The cost of admission is approximately €10 per person.

Maison Carrée A Roman Architectural Gem

- At Maison Carrée, a magnificently preserved Roman temple, immerse yourself in architectural magnificence.
- Admire the magnificent sculptures and detailed details of Corinthian columns.
- Discover the temple's evolution from a sanctuary to a museum over time.

The cost of admission is approximately €6 per person.

Day 2
Jardins de la Fontaine and Markets Locals

Jardins de la Fontaine's Natural Tranquility

- Stroll around the Jardins de la Fontaine, a lovely garden with fountains, sculptures, and lush foliage.
- Climb to the peak for panoramic views of the city and Diana's Temple.
- Enjoy a peaceful respite from city life among ancient ruins.

Admission is free.

Local Markets For A Gastronomic and Creative Experience

- Participate in the lively ambiance of Nimes' local markets, such as Les Halles de Nimes.
- Enjoy a sensory experience with stalls selling fresh produce, cheeses, wines, and handcrafted crafts.
- Interact with local sellers while collecting items for a picnic or culinary experience.

Spending varies depending on purchases.

Nîmoise Delicacies And Culinary Temptations

Nîmes Brandade
A Creamy Cod Delight

- Brandade de Nîmes is a classic meal that combines salt fish, olive oil, and garlic.

- Enjoy the creamy texture and rich flavors, which are frequently eaten with bread or vegetables.

Price per serving: €10 - €15.

Picholine Olives
A Snack from the Mediterranean
- Picholine olives, a local variety famed for their plumpness and particular flavor, are delicious.
- Combine them with area wines to create a delectable Mediterranean tasting experience.

Price: Around €5 per portion.

Accommodation options range from charming bed and breakfasts to modern hotels.

Lovely B&Bs
La Maison d'Élise
La Maison d'Élise, a beautiful Bed & Breakfast with rustic decor welcomes you, In a cozy atmosphere where you can enjoy customized service and cooked breakfasts.

The price each night begins at €80.

Hotel Imperator For Modern Comfort
Enjoy the modern comforts of Hotel Imperator, a blend of history and modernity.

Enjoy well-appointed rooms, spa services, and delectable eating selections.
Price per night begins at €150.

Chapter 9

Hidden Treasures and Countryside Getaways

Beyond the Main Cities

Exploring-Off The Beaten Paths

France's allure stretches far beyond its famed cities. Traveling to the countryside promises a new type of charm, one that reveals hidden treasures and calm getaways that frequently go unnoticed in the middle of metropolitan beauty.

In this chapter, we will travel through the rustic villages, vineyard-laden landscapes, and exquisite rural settings of Provence, searching for hidden treasures.

Rustic Villages

Les Baux-de-Provence and Lourmarin

Les Baux-de-Provence and Lourmarin, two charming villages in the heart of Provence, each give a distinct view into the region's rich cultural tapestry and natural splendor.

Les Baux-de-Provence
Perched on a rocky outcrop, Les Baux-de-Provence appears to have sprung from the pages of a fairy tale. It is an amazing destination due to its medieval architecture, tiny alleyways, and beautiful views of the Alpilles mountains.

The massive ruins of Château des Baux provide an intriguing voyage through history, while the Carrières de Lumières—a former limestone quarry—transforms into an immersive art environment, with multimedia shows bringing iconic artworks to life on the quarry's colossal walls.

Lourmarin
In contrast to the spectacular heights of Les Baux, Lourmarin emits a gentler charm. This charming village in the Luberon mountains emanates a lovely atmosphere.

The Renaissance castle, with its magnificent façade and lush grounds, attests to the historical significance of Lourmarin. Visitors can enjoy artisan boutiques, quaint cafés, and a weekly market that celebrates the flavors of Provence while strolling through its cobbled alleys shaded by plane trees.

Côtes du Rhône Wine Route Adventure

The Côtes du Rhône region is a must-see on any countryside trip for wine connoisseurs. This region, which stretches along the Rhône River, is well-known for its vineyards, which produce some of France's finest wines.

Exploring the wine road here is a sensory experience unlike any other. The tour leads you past vineyard-dotted undulating hills, where you may drink excellent wines in family-owned wineries and centuries-old cellars.

The region's moderate temperature and diversified geography produce a wide range of wines, from strong reds to delicate whites. Visit Châteauneuf-du-Pape, known for its robust red blends, and experience the flavors while overlooking the magnificent scenery.

Relaxation in Saint-Rémy-de-Provence

Saint-Rémy-de-Provence is a relaxing and inspiring destination. Vincent van Gogh's most famous works were born in this lovely Provençal village.

Many of his masterpieces were inspired by the surrounding landscape, and tourists can follow in his footsteps by following the Van Gogh Trail, which leads to the sights that inspired him.

The town itself is a beautiful combination of history and modern conveniences. Its cobblestone lanes weave around lively squares and are lined with stores, art galleries, and traditional cafés.

A must-see is the tranquil Monastery Saint-Paul de Mausole, where van Gogh sought therapy and created some of his art. The hues of Provence come alive as the sun sets, throwing a warm glow across the landscape.

Budget-Friendly Charm

Stays in Idyllic Rural Settings
One of the most enticing parts of countryside getaways is the opportunity to disengage from the

outside world and relax in peaceful settings. Accommodation options in Provence's rural settings range from small bed and breakfasts to picturesque cottages, with alternatives to suit a variety of budgets.

Agriturismos
Consider staying in an agriturismo, which is a farmhouse that has been turned into guest accommodations.

These hotels allow you to immerse yourself in the agricultural heritage of the region while still providing comfortable conveniences.

Many agriturismos serve home-cooked meals made with locally obtained products, giving guests a true flavor of Provençal cuisine. And you my friend will be in for a treat!

Itinerary for the Hidden Treasures and Countryside Getaways

Day 1
Provence' Rustic Villages - Les Baux-de-Provence and Lourmarin

Morning
After breakfast, take a picturesque drive to Les Baux-de-Provence, a medieval town located on a rocky mountaintop.

Wander through small cobblestone alleyways, observe well-preserved ancient architecture, and visit the remains of Château des Baux-de-Provence. The castle admission fee is approximately €10 per person.

Afternoon
Drive to Lourmarin in the afternoon, a lovely village famed for its colorful markets and creative ambiance.

Enjoy a leisurely lunch at a nearby café; a modest but good meal may cost between €15 and €20 per person. After that, visit the Lourmarin Castle, which costs about €6 to enter.

Evening
Take in the peaceful atmosphere of the villages as you stroll through the streets in the evening light. Consider a low-cost meal at a nearby restaurant, with rates ranging from €20 to €30 per person.

Day 2

Côtes du Rhône Wine Route Adventure

Morning

Take a lovely drive through the Côtes du Rhône wine region, which is famous for its vineyard-covered scenery.

Visit local vineyards for tastings; pricing vary, but plan on spending €10-15 per taste. Discover the art of winemaking while indulging in regional delicacies.

Afternoon

Relax with a picnic among the vines. Local markets sell fresh produce, bread, cheese, and wine for roughly €20-25 for a delicious spread.

Evening

Consider going to a traditional Provençal restaurant in the countryside for dinner. A three-course lunch might cost between €30 and €40 per person. Enjoy the native cuisine while admiring the sights.

Day 3

Saint-Rémy-de-Provence Relaxation Retreat

Morning

When you arrive in Saint-Rémy-de-Provence in the morning, check into a delightful bed and breakfast.

Prices vary, but for comfortable lodging, budget roughly €70-100 per night.

Afternoon
Visit the Monastery of Saint-Paul de Mausole, where Van Gogh once sought inspiration. The cost of admission is approximately €5.

Spend the afternoon browsing the stores and galleries in town, or unwind at a neighborhood café.

Evening
Relax at your B&B with a leisurely dinner or travel into town for some traditional Provençal food. Prices per person might range from €25 to €40.

The Cost Prices For Budget-Friendly Charm: Stays in Idyllic Rural Settings
Consider staying in gorgeous rural surroundings for an immersive experience throughout your journey:

Farmhouse Appeal Of The Agriturismos
- Where you'd discover the rustic appeal of a refurbished farmhouse.

- Prices here vary greatly depending on location and amenities, but plan on spending €60-120 per night.

Nice Cottages

- Choose a nice cottage that is surrounded by nature for a surreal experience.

- Prices range from €50 to €100 per night and include comfort and solitude.

- Discover modest guest houses that provide individual hospitality. Prices per night, including breakfast, can range between €70 and €100.

Chapter 10

Useful Informations For Tourist

Trends And Highlights To Look Forward-To

As you plan your trip to Southern France, it is critical to stay up to date on the current travel trends and anticipated highlights. This chapter will provide insights into emerging trends as well as showcase some of the region's must-see sites.

Travel Trends

Southern France has embraced sustainable tourism methods as travelers grow increasingly concerned of their environmental impact. There are numerous ways to reduce your carbon footprint, ranging from eco-friendly hotels to locally sourced dining options.

Culinary Exploration: Southern France is a culinary paradise, and immersive food excursions are becoming increasingly popular.

Consider taking cooking courses or going on culinary tours to sample traditional dishes like Bouillabaisse or Ratatouille and have a better understanding of local cuisine.

Off-the-Beaten-Paths
In addition to renowned tourist destinations, there is a growing interest in discovering hidden gems and lesser-known communities.

For a more authentic experience, including small villages like Eze or Saint-Paul-de-Vence in your itinerary.

Highlights to be expected

Provence's Lavender Fields
The famed lavender fields that bloom in Provence during the summer are a stunning sight. Visit between June and August to photograph the vivid purple sceneries of the Valensole Plateau.

Pont du Gard
A UNESCO World Heritage Site and engineering marvel, the Pont du Gard is a historic Roman aqueduct. Explore its history and take in the scenic surrounds, which frequently hold cultural events.

Calanques National Park

The Calanques are a haven for nature lovers, with rocky cliffs, turquoise waterways, and hiking routes. For a memorable experience, take a boat cruise or hike to hidden beaches.

Essential Websites, Apps, Maps and Travel Resources

Navigating the planning process is made easier by the availability of numerous resources that provide insights and guidance.

Websites

TripAdvisor: Read reviews, uncover top-rated attractions, and receive recommendations from fellow visitors on where to go.

Apps

Google Maps: An invaluable navigation tool that can help you find attractions, restaurants, and lodging.

Duolingo: Before your vacation, brush up on your French language abilities to improve your interactions with locals.

Making Your Own Customized Itinerary

And Customizing Your Southern France Experience

Making a well-rounded schedule guarantees that you get the most out of your time in Southern France. Here's a rough guide to creating and adding your own itinerary

Marseille (Days 1-3)
- Explore the Old Port and dine at local restaurants serving fresh seafood.

- For panoramic views of the city, go to the Basilique Notre-Dame de la Garde.

- Discover Marseille's history at the Museum of European and Mediterranean Civilizations (MuCEM).

Day 4 to 6: Provence
- Immerse yourself in Valensole's lavender fields.
- Discover Aix-en-Provence's lovely town and vibrant markets.

- Visit Avignon's Palais des Papes, a majestic medieval palace.

7th to 10th day: French Riviera

- *Relax on Nice's beaches and walk along the Promenade des Anglais.*

- *Explore Saint-Paul-de-Vence creative heritage and its numerous galleries.*

- *Discover Monaco's glitz and elegance, including the Casino Monte-Carlo.*

Budget Management
For Long-Term Travel Considerations
Effective money management provides a stress-free and joyful journey.

Accommodation
Budget: *Hostels and budget hotels range in price from €30 to €50 per night.*

Comfortable hotels and guesthouses *range in price from €80 to €150 per night.*

High-end resorts and boutique hotels *can cost more than €200 per night.*

Meals
Street food and cafes: *a lunch will cost you between €10 and €20.*

Mid-range restaurants: *Expect to pay between €30 and €50 per person.*

Fine dining: *A meal at a Michelin-starred restaurant can cost up to €100 per person.*

Transport
Trains: *Depending on the distance, train travel between cities costs between €20 and €60.*

Buses: *Intercity buses are a cost-effective choice, with fares ranging from €15 to €30.*

Local transportation: *In cities, public transportation costs about €1.50-€2 each ride.*

Activities
Museums and attractions: *Admission fees range from €5 to €15.*

Guided tours: *Depending on the activity, guided tours can range in price from €20 to €50 per person.*

Hiking and boat tours, *for example, might cost between €20 and €80.*

Tourist Information Centres

Office de Tourisme de Nice

(Nice Tourist Office)
Address: 5 Promenade des Anglais, 06000 Nice, France
Phone: +33 4 92 14 46 14
Website: nice-tourism.com

Marseille Tourist Office

(Office de Tourisme et des Congrès de Marseille)
Address: 11 La Canebière, 13001 Marseille, France
Phone: +33 826 500 500
Website: marseille-tourisme.com

Office de Tourisme de Bordeaux Métropole

(Bordeaux Tourist Office)
Address: 12 Cours du 30 Juillet, 33000 Bordeaux, France
Phone: +33 5 56 00 66 00
Website: bordeaux-tourism.co.uk

Toulouse Tourist Office

(Office de Tourisme de Toulouse)
Address: Donjon du Capitole, Square Charles de Gaulle, 31080 Toulouse, France
Phone: +33 5 61 11 02 22
Website: toulouse-visit.com

Avignon Tourist Office

(Office de Tourisme d'Avignon)
Address: Palais des Papes, Place du Palais des Papes, 84000 Avignon, France
Phone: +33 4 32 74 32 74
Website: avignon-tourisme.com

Cannes Tourist Office

(Office de Tourisme de Cannes)
Address: Palais des Festivals et des Congrès, 1 Boulevard de la Croisette, 06400 Cannes, France
Phone: +33 4 92 99 84 22
Website: cannes-destination.com

Aix-en-Provence Tourist Office

(Office de Tourisme d'Aix-en-Provence)
Address: Les Allées Provençales, 300 Avenue Giuseppe Verdi, 13605 Aix-en-Provence, France

Phone: +33 4 42 161 161
Website: aixenprovencetourism.com

Montpellier Tourist Office

(Office de Tourisme et des Congrès de Montpellier)
Address: 30 Allée Jean de Lattre de Tassigny, 34000 Montpellier, France
Phone: +33 4 67 60 60 60
Website: ot-montpellier.fr

Made in the USA
Middletown, DE
18 February 2024

49981336R00061